Gloved Against Blood

GLOVED AGAINST BLOOD

CINDY VEACH

CavanKerry ❖ Press LTD.

CavanKerry Press Ltd.
Fort Lee, New Jersey
www.cavankerrypress.org

Publisher's Cataloging-In-Publication Data
(Prepared by The Donohue Group, Inc.)
Names: Veach, Cindy.
Title: Gloved against blood / Cindy Veach.
Description: First edition. | Fort Lee, New Jersey : CavanKerry Press Ltd., 2017.
Identifiers: ISBN 978-1-933880-64-8
Subjects: LCSH: Women textile workers—Massachusetts—Lowell—History—19th century—Poetry. | Women immigrants—New England—History—19th century—Poetry. | Women—New England—Social conditions—19th century—Poetry. | Slaves—Southern States—History—19th century—Poetry. | Exploitation—Poetry.
Classification: LCC PS3622.E33 G56 2017 | DDC 811/.6—dc23

Cover photograph courtesy of January Gill O'Neil.
Photo on pages ii–iii courtesy of the Library of Congress, Prints & Photographs Division, LC-DIG-nclc-03083

Cover and interior text design by Ryan Scheife, Mayfly Design

First Edition 2017, Printed in the United States of America

EMERGING VOICES
CavanKerry❧Press

CavanKerry Press is dedicated to springboarding the careers of previously unpublished, early, and mid-career poets by bringing to print two to three Emerging Voices annually. Manuscripts are selected from open submission; CavanKerry Press does not conduct competitions.

CavanKerry Press is grateful for the support it receives from the New Jersey State Council on the Arts.

For my parents
Carson Ward Veach & Pauline Paquereau Veach

In memory of Mary Anne Jalbert Paquereau & Marie Delorme Jalbert

For we are our loom.
—MARCEL PROUST

Contents

Now I Must Forget

Foreword

There are moments when poems can breathe a deeper meaning into our lives, when they strike something profound in us, remind us of a truth we've always known. Cindy Veach's debut collection, *Gloved Against Blood*, is one such occasion. Her words enter us with preciseness and an attentiveness to sublime detail. Her poems take my breath away.

The poet's landscapes explore the patriarchal textile mills of Lowell, Massachusetts, and the women who labored in them. These young women sought economic independence and freedom, but it came at a price. Veach opens a window on this 19th-century industry that was fueled by the blood and sweat of exploited mill girls and enslaved African Americans in the South. What does it mean to be a woman, to work for independence, to make hard choices, and to live on the margins?

Like a cloth pulled taut, the poet pushes the ordinary language beyond the extraordinary into the realm of art. She uses language to shape the story of mill girls into something completely new and unique. These poems have texture and in the book's first section, "Community," she pulls this harsh history into the weft and warp of the loom.

> ...How they
> sucked thread through the eye of their foot-long wooden shuttles
> that fed the cotton to the looms. How they called that quick motion
> of their lips "the kiss of death."

Veach plays within the music of poetic conventions of repetition, anaphora, and enjambment to remake them in her own unique vision.

In "Ordinary Art," the poem seeks to reconcile the past with the continuum of illness:

What happens now

as you disappear
    as she did

brain cell by brain cell—
    is that our story?

There is nothing ordinary about this extraordinary book. These quiet yet powerful poems deepen the questions of what we pass along from generation to generation, the lives fitting into lives, the hands that labor, the eyes that follow and observe and learn and pass on, seamlessly moving from past to present and back again. Nothing escapes the needle's path, as in this passage from the poem "Predators."

I've wandered online
    searching for my lineage,

that unquiet room
    of looms,

the girls who drove them—

And from another section, a line that lends itself to the title.

And my grandmother
    whose county fair afghan,

decades in the making, was disqualified
    by a cross-stitch mistake.

And what of her cracked
    hands,

gloved against blood,
    her bad marriage?

Veach masterfully captures a timeline of work life with firsthand and secondhand accounts, while affirming that women's work is more than trifles. These poems honor tradition with its rich detail and love of language. In the process, her work celebrates the best of our American poetic tradition. Veach breathes life into these family poems, which intensifies as the speaker does the close work of making the old world new again.

It is an unattainable, dreamed-of thing to truly know one's history. But this is what Veach does every time on the page, to envision the past with fresh eyes, where light and dark and every shade of gray is welcomed. History becomes the background—the tapestry—for those moments of personal revelation.

> Mother of pearl and bone buttons,
>   Coats & Clark thread.
>
> I'd sort and touch every notion
>   in her basket
>
> with its silk loops for thimbles
>   and pine posts for bobbins.

Colloquial and without artifice, the poet, Cindy Veach, is all "Mother of pearl and bone buttons." Even when she considers the past—examines what we assume is women's work—it is all truth. There's a willful refusal not to look away from harsh truths of love, loss, divorce, even cruelty. And yet, there is an appreciation for the work, a pride that is bright and breathing on the page.

—JANUARY GILL O'NEIL

Gloved Against Blood

Community

How It Resists

And sometimes it's too much—

    these aisles of crowded looms,

their stanchions of white thread

    spooling like udders,

my needy shuttles

    of flowering dogwood—

for its hardness, for how it resists

    splintering, for the way it loves

to be polished smooth—

    some days

the floor slants,

    the room seems cockeyed,

light muddles,

    too slim for eyes

to see the eye—

    and the whole mill howls

as if cotton were milk—

    the way two mirrors held just right

create an infinity of I—

Earthlings

Things that are beautiful, and die.
—LAURA KASISCHKE

On a plane we say souls—
    one hundred souls aboard

not the same with cars
    as if proximity to earth negates

the idea that we are more
    beautiful than matter.

Is that why down here the trooper covers
    the body with a sheet—

and two deer, side by side
    on the shoulder of the highway

legs splayed like clothespins
    that lost their grip

are emptied carcasses filling
    with pyramids of new snow

feather weight?
    The plow blade sparks blue

when it finds pavement
    flickers.

These balding, out-of-balance tires
    carry us—

each rotation
    stitched to the next

if luck holds
    random and catch as catch can

but viable viable
    here on earth

and nowhere else
    and nowhere next.

Great Red Wall

This is the Merrimack, the Charles, the Concord.
And this—the red brick of mills,
the home of warp and weft
that lured them from their failing farms
to toil cotton into cloth thirteen hours a day.
And this—red brick on brick on brick
is all that's left of sweat and linty lungs.
Can you see them years later—in these offices,
these cubicles, these cute boutiques
with clothes made in Bangladesh
or sitting in the hip cafés that sell espresso
fifteen ways? Here is where they spent
their days. Where factory bells rang
come and *done*.

Theft

How I came down from Quebec to work in the mills—
How I never imagined it would be such hell. How industry.
How factory bell. How many miles of cloth I conjured
from the bloody cotton. How my eyes couldn't get enough
of the one window—the Great Out There. How I lied—
about a cloudless sky; there was one solitary cloud
far up in the cerulean vault. How I schemed to leave—
steal my wages instead of sending them back home
to make a gentleman of my brother—
my heart fluttered, like a prisoned bird
with painful longings for an unchecked flight—
how your grandmother, mother, you, how your daughter—
because I came here. Because I did not flee.

Drawn

The light so small

when you woke to say goodbye

to your country,

to walk years in darkness

to and from the factory, texture

a life from mill work—

Tell me, what brought you

to place your foot

on the treadle,

to thrum and thrum

until poverty was a phantom?

And what of the visions

you threaded your shuttle

with? Please

speak to the warp

and the weft—

that which is thrown across

that which is drawn through.

How a Community of Women

Resolved, That we will not go back into the mills to work
unless our wages are continued...as they have been.
Resolved, That none of us will go back, unless they receive us all as one.
Resolved, That if any have not money enough to carry them home,
they shall be supplied.
　　　—BOSTON EVENING TRANSCRIPT, FEBRUARY 18, 1834

How my French Canadian great-grandmother and great-great-aunts
toiled thirteen hours a day in the textile mills of Lowell, Massachusetts.
How weak the light when they left the boardinghouse each morning.
How screaming starlings flash mobbed them along the way. How they
sucked thread through the eye of their foot-long wooden shuttles
that fed the cotton to the looms. How they called that quick motion
of their lips "the kiss of death." How they could not converse over the
cacophonic, clickety-click, clickety-clack of five-hundred howling
looms. How they walked back in ear-ringing darkness, had dinner,
then took up their needlework—crochet, crewel, cross-stitch, knitting,
mending, quilting, darning—close work, women's work. My mother
taught me, her mother taught her, her mother taught her.

Thimbleful

If the mill girl in the daguerreotype is a stranger
then this nine-patch is an old friend.
If an ankle is as ambitious as an argument
then success is a juggernaut.
If a bulldozer acts like an elephant,
if ice is as slippery as thieves
then spring peepers are singing
insincere condolences
full steam ahead like a cruise ship
headed for disaster—
or ice is garlands of water
stopped in time is time
while an elephant is nature's bulldozer
and success is as sweet and sour as living
for the same reason ankles are boomerangs
and this quilt reminds me
of the silver and gold filigreed thimble
that belonged to my great-grandmother, grandmother, mother—
the way it protects me from the quick stick
of sharps and betweens
at the same time it is a vessel, repository, crèche
for the spiraled remnants of their making.

Coming to Massachusetts

Imagine
the sky pink

the morning Mémé left Quebec
for a mill job in Massachusetts.

Imagine
so many reasons to go—

worn land, lean crops, debt.

And not to go—
her family, her country, her root tongue.

Imagine
Mémé before the only image

that exists, a daguerreotype—

younger,
maybe two small trunks, a stoic look back,

one hand still waving.

Notions

There is a hierarchy in the arts: decorative art at the bottom,
and the human form at the top. Because we are men.
— LE CORBUSIER AND AMÉDÉE OZENFANT, 1918

Mother of pearl and bone buttons,
    Coats & Clark thread.

I'd sort and touch every notion
    in her basket

with its silk loops for thimbles
    and pine posts for bobbins.

First day of school outfits, hems,
    elbow and knee patches she conjured

from that basket.
    I need some notions

meant a trip to Woolworth's—
    ice cream at the soda fountain for me,

every flavor of rickrack, bias tape, grosgrain
    for her. How she could darn

socks by the hour,
    create buttonholes by hand,

always kept her notions
    organized, neat

so she could find what she needed—
    a rhinestone button, safety

pins, scarlet embroidery floss
    to stitch I love you.

She said a woman
    could never have enough—

fabric could unravel, split, fray,
    but a woman with notions

could mend what was torn—
    make it like new

button up
    against his absence.

Triptych: Travaux d'Aiguille

. . . a spot where a story now gone has ridden.
The yarn spinning free.
                    —JORIE GRAHAM

I. Nanny

She could handle the finest yarn—when it tried to fly away
she made it stay. Wrapped it tight around two fingers

                    pulled it over, under—

knit purl knit purl. Her needles clicked. If she dropped a stitch
she'd pick it up, quick. If she found a mistake she'd rip the piece

all the way back and start over. Evenings were for needlework—
passing the time, she'd say. *Busy work,* my father said. She left

school in 8th grade. The oldest girl—she had to care for baby Rose.

II. Penelope (*'pene' the Greek noun for 'thread'*)

Nowhere in the literature is the shroud described—size, variegation,
gauge, thread (silk, linen, cotton)—

only the deed

itself. Penelope, weaving by day, unweaving by night. Modern
psychology has named this, *perpetual activity*

without progress. A condition agnostic of gender. But she was not
a sufferer—this weaver of strategies. And this to avoid capture. To thwart

she claimed the distaff and the shuttle.

III. Mémé

I've seen the steps she climbed each morning to begin another day
in the mill. They spiral like a beaded periwinkle

                    toward a far-off rectangle

of light. Three years she threw the shuttle through the web
of cotton threads before she stopped for him. And then the thirteen

births. The lost one's name was Rose. He shuttled between women.
The close work kept her calm. She bore the thimble well

and climbed the steps each morning.

My Mother Is Forgetting

And why no stars tonight?
Every crumb swept clean
no finding her way back
to that
home she left
this morning.

Or was it last evening
she lost her way
and knelt at the door
without keys—

let me in.

And now a cloud sea comes
and covers up
the life she's built

until memories evaporate
every moment a new moon.
This is when I turn

weary of our journey
and look up and up
past her eyes, past her long
fingers of light

we are about to lose.

Blood From My Finger

This Threshold He Did Not Carry Her Across

Evil spirits, in a last-ditch effort to curse the couple, hovered at the threshold,
so the bride had to be lifted to ensure that the spirits couldn't enter her body
through the soles of her feet.

—THEKNOT.COM

Not literal this threshold, two parts wild animal—
something to be wrangled with—one part fir,
smattered with dents, and she a sucker
for first impressions, let him break her
hymen, spooling blood, the only one. Fir,
a soft wood, pale yellow, some would say
wan, the grain and knots right at the surface,
ill-suited for the soles of shoes coming
and going, mostly the cursed going.

Thirteen Hours of Labor Daily

Now isn't it a pity | Such a pretty girl as I
Should be sent to the factory | To pine away and die.
—LETTERS FROM SUSAN, THE LOWELL OFFERING

We have lately visited Lowell
We went through the mills
We talked to a large number of operatives
We learned they work thirteen hours a day daylight to dark
    thirty minutes for breakfast
    thirty minutes for dinner
    when Capital has got thirteen hours of labor daily out of a being
    it can get nothing more
We entered into the large rooms
    when the looms were at work—four hundred feet long
    and seventy broad—five hundred looms
    when Capital has got thirteen hours of labor daily out of a being
    it can get nothing more
We were struck on first entering
    as something frightful and infernal for it seemed
    such an atrocious violation of one of the faculties
    of the human soul
    when Capital has got thirteen hours of labor daily out of a being
    it can get nothing more
We saw the girls attend upon an average three looms many four
We observed the atmosphere in such a room cannot of course be pure
    charged with cotton filaments and dust
    when Capital has got thirteen hours of labor daily out of a being
    it can get nothing more
We saw the windows were down

We asked the reason
    a young woman said when the wind blew
    the threads did not work so well
    when Capital has got thirteen hours of labor daily out of a being
    it can get nothing more

After the First Week

    I'm getting used
to the hurry of things—
    obeying the bells,
banter of a room of looms
    set end to end to end,
barefoot doffers
    running up the aisles,
switching out our bobbins—
    the skinny mites swarm in
they climb the looms to reach.
    How lithe their tiny fingers.
In between the boss lets them play
    marbles in the mill-yard.
I hear them tell each other small
    hopes, the one who does the shawl dance
in the alley plans to run away,
    join the circus—be a lion tamer,
we all have aspirations—
    as the clattering machines
wring our ears all day.

Regulations to Be Observed by All

Persons employed the overseers are to be always watching all

They are to see all

And keep correct account of all

Persons in the employ are to observe all

The regulations not to be absent without the consent of the overseer all

Persons entering into the employment are considered all

Engaged for twelve months and those who leave sooner or all

Who do not comply with all

These regulations will all

Not be entitled to regular discharge the company will not employ all

Who are habitually absent from public worship on the Sabbath all

Known to be guilty of immorality all

Who shall take any yarn cloth or other article will be considered guilty all

These regulations are considered part of the contract with which all

Persons entering into employment engage to comply with all

Curating My Grandfather

Are those his eyes
    blinking over her oatmeal,

    his hand, a confluence of blue
        tributaries, pushing the white bangs

off her face?
    How do you curate

    a man who vanished
        into thin air?

Even the whale found floating
    in Boston Harbor last month

    eventually wound up on a beach
        in Rockport.

When I ask my mother what she remembers
    she says there is nothing

    to forget. And I see that she's navigated
        these waters without him

for eighty-six years. This doesn't stop me
    from believing that to study her face,

    which is my face, is to study
        his. Our histories

at cross-purposes—
    trying to be better this time around, to

never leave. I ask myself,
     if it was his hand that guided my brother

toward the bottle, falling in love with its slim
     cool neck? He drowned

     and came back until he could not.
          And now we are two

women alone—the same twin cheekbones
     and almond eyes. I've been practicing my French

     I tell her. *Look*, she says pointing—
          an ibis. All legs and elegance at the edge—

But whose eyes? Blinking
     behind snow-white bangs.

Sewing Lessons

How many evenings, dishes done, they sit in the parlor
stitching. How many times the needle kisses her finger,

red beading the muslin fabric. How she mimics
the angle of Mémé's needle, tautness of her thread.

How's she's getting used to the thimble. The way it's clumsy—
stops feeling. How she has plans for each remnant,

ribbon, embroidery floss in the basket. How to make
a knot that won't pull through the sheerest cloth.

Dear Francis Cabot Lowell

*—founder of the first textile mill that transformed raw cotton into cloth under
one roof increasing productivity and the demand for cotton.*

How is it you don't see all down the row,
blood bobbins blood bobbins all down the row?

I've heard fields of white bolls, each puff turned up
to the sun, are beautiful by the row.

But at what price this *accursed fibre*
that threads your looms, your looms all in a row?

Every day *I feel that I am sinning*
against the light to stay still in a row.

Turn those fields ten thousand times—*the blood of*
souls in bondage will thicken by the row.

Francis, you are the sin—not these cloven,
white perennials planted in a row.

They bleed I weave. I weave they bleed. Why can't
you see—blood threads your looms all down the row?

Lowell Cloth Narratives

Based on Ex-Slave Narratives conducted by the Works Progress Administration (WPA) in the 1930s. Lowell cloth was a "generic" term for cheap, coarse cotton cloth, produced originally in the textile mills of Waltham, later Lowell.

State: Arkansas Interviewee: Bear, Dina (in italics)

I was born in slavery time—a world away
*we wove we wove away. I was born in the field
under a tree.* Thirteen hours a day we toiled
cotton into cloth. *People wore home-made
what I mean homespun and lowell clothes.*
It snowed in our lungs and every window
shut. *My dresses was called mother
hubbards.* We passed abolitionist poems
from loom to loom. *I was too young
to remember anything about slavery*—
blood and sweat blood and sweat. *I went
barefoot until I was a young missie.* We
signed the petitions. *Folk did not know
how we was made.*

State: Arkansas Interviewee: Tatum, Fannie (in italics)

I wasn't allowed to sat at the table—a world away
we wove we wove away. *I et on the edge*
of the porch with the dogs with my fingers—
thirteen hours a day we toiled cotton
into cloth. *I wore two pieces, a lowell underskirt*
and a lowell dress, bachelor brogans and sacks
and rags wrapped around my legs. It snowed
in our lungs and every window shut. *At ten*
I started splitting rails—*my task was two hundred*
a day. We passed abolitionist poems from loom
to loom. *If I didn't cut them I got a beating*—
blood and sweat blood and sweat. *I didn't know*
what a coat was. We signed the petitions. *My hat*
was rag tied on my head.

State: Oklahoma Interviewee: Anderson, Sam (in italics)

We slaves live in de quarters—a world away
we wove we wove away. *Beds made
out of wood with shuck and moss
mattress.* Thirteen hours a day we toiled
cotton into cloth. *We always put de moss
in hot water so it don't grow.* It snowed
in our lungs and every window shut. *I wore
a shirt until I was ten years old.* We passed
abolitionist poems from loom to loom.
Shirts was made of old lowell—blood
and sweat blood and sweat. *Nothing different
on Sunday only clean clothes.* We signed
the petitions. *They was split up de sides
so dey would sail out behind when you ran.*

Absent

He left
    not as leaves

leave—anticipated,
    lauded, each scarlet

boutonnièred
    usher cartwheeling,

top spinning,
    down,

into bright
    spoils heaped

at our feet—
    not as something

erased
    where then the branches,

emptied, brim over
    with blue—

but as a tree
    splits,

cleaved
    to the quick

roots
    uprooted

ants, aphids, nematodes
    disowned

in the dark
    in the eye

of it—

Field Trip: Boott Cotton Mills

Is it too much to hope
    for a strand of you?

It's possible
    I was born imprinted

beginning with *loom*
    from the old word *gelōme*

stitched beside my fate line
    so I may salvage our history:

what you wished for, why
    you came. I wish

to open my hand and find you
    my daughter's age

running three or four looms,
    deaf to the clatter,

heddles and shuttles ringing ears
    thirteen hours a day: I tell her,

"your great-great-grandmother emigrated
    from Canada to work in those mills"—

after she comes home from school
    with a swatch of cloth she wove

as I finger its flawed lines.
    I must teach her how

as we pass through the eye
    of our coming and going

that you may lead
    us to the *fell*

the point where the warp & weft
    become cloth—

Like Her

Nanny's gloves gleamed white cotton
    three neat pintucks

down the back.
    She wore them as she worked

on the afghan.
    Her hands were dry—cracks

could catch, could snag,
    sometimes even blood—

the gloves gave an extra
    measure of precaution.

I wondered how she could
    work like that.

Sunday nights watching Ed Sullivan
    counting and placing markers,

close work—the yarn,
    for the background panels

where she would cross-stitch
    tea roses

through my childhood,
    the color of bone, ecru, eggshell.

She never talked about her loss
    of faith—

how she left the Church
    decades after he walked out.

When my own hands cracked, raw
    from upstate winters,

she rubbed them with Vaseline
    offered a pair of her gloves.

Everything she touched
    was a kind of purpose prayer.

The afghan, draped over
    the back of the divan

in my mother's den
    turns yellow—

I finger a single rose,
    remember how she kept

track on a scrap of paper
    in groups of five.

I lose count, start over—
    like her I've stopped believing.

The Other Woman

My grandfather did not come back
instead he sent his girlfriend knock-
knocking on the door to ask *please*
grant him a divorce. My mother,
age two, peek-a-booed
with this visitor in camel-hair coat
with painted nails. And my young
grandmother in her thin housedress
a pocketful of rosary beads, gold-plated
crucifix tap-tapped on her collarbone
like a metronome. For she believed
believed. Read her *Maryknolls*, went
to daily mass, confessed to the gauzy man
shadow who at the end mimed his blessing
making of his hand a steeple that knifed the air
she breathed as he pronounced her penance—
which could erase every black mark
but one. No, no, not for any number
of Our Fathers. This she knew
knew and never questioned
even at the moment the softly
made-up other woman stood before her
both feet firmly planted on the threshold
mouthing—*please*.

Breakfast on the Lanai with My Mother

I walk early, bring her back photographs
    of spiderwebs spun overnight

strung between palms,
    a banyan tree's aerial prop root

tied in a French knot,
    a great white egret stalking

an anole for breakfast,
    shock of green

waggling in its orange beak;
    she brings me marmalade

and memory—

    As a girl
I loved to go to Mémé's house.

    She had a toilette with pull chain
an upright piano she let me play

    and a backyard garden, un jardin potager,
flush with tomatoes, cucumbers, and squash.

    In her kitchen there was a black stove
where she used to burn my toast.

Now I Must Forget

December Selves

What of this place
    that is more than the rain
        and fog which tethers

sky to earth or earth to sky
    so there is no line
        no easy demarcation

the jumping-off point
    unclear—is it there?
        Not there?

And what of the moths
    who have returned
        swaddling the door

with their December selves.
    They want to come in
        can't refuse the light

and once inside fold their wings
    sleep until spring
        turns them to soot.

In the Basilica
    the faithful kneel
        before the mummified pope—

the body so
    small, so overwhelmed
        by cardinal

robes, stiff
    gold trim, skull-
        cap pulled

to his brow
    over the ears,
        the face

nothing
    but a triangle
        of ruined cloth—

Accent

With some exceptions the Canadian French are the Chinese of the Eastern States.
—CARROLL D. WRIGHT, "UNIFORM HOURS OF LABOR"

It's true my people were scabs
who crossed picket lines in the dark,
weren't afraid to turn
fingers into bone or ruin
their hearing from the din
of screeching looms.
French filled the home
where my grandmother was born
and raised—white clapboard
with a glassed-in porch
on a curving street.
She drove me past
when she still drove.
Rough times in Lowell
after the mills shut down.
I made fun of her Yankee accent—
cah and *yahd.*
She worked hard to talk like that.

French Seams

The little useless seam, the idle patch
. . . this pretty futile seam.
—ALICE MOORE DUNBAR-NELSON

From Nanny Paquereau
    I learned to sew French seams—

seams that hide raw edges
    within the seam itself.

Seams that won't unravel,
    that are neat,

even on the wrong side—
    finished she'd say.

Seams that take planning, accurate
    estimating, extra fabric—

each one folded over twice—
    making allowances she called it.

Hers were meticulous, unrivaled.
    They could be counted on

to hold. They never ripped or frayed.
    Still, the marriage unraveled early.

She had to stitch shoes
    at McElwin's in Nashua

and raise a latchkey kid.
    When Social Security

could not sustain her
    she came to live with us.

Garter-stitch dishrags all she could manage
    when senility set in.

From Nanny Paquereau
    I learned to hide raw edges

within the seam itself
    each one folded over twice—

making allowances she called it.
    Even on the wrong side

I would not rip or fray.
    I would be counted on

to hold. I would be neat,
    meticulous, unrivaled.

It would take planning, accurate
    estimating, extra fabric—

Still, the marriage raveled
    I had to stitch and stitch

fold and fold and fold
    all that extra yardage

I could not salvage us—
    finished she'd say.

Math Lessons

Up at the blackboard
the last one standing—

a whole class waiting
for me to get it.

Later, my mother sat me down
at the electrical spool table

she'd painted glossy
black like a piano

without keys. Tornado
of torn paper, snapped

pencils—I could not listen.
Would not try.

Old hot head. I yelled
and stomped, fisted the table.

No degree—she was all smarts
and patience. I was snippy, girl

mean, refused her help,
then hated myself—*dal segno.*

When I visit her now,
I walk the circle of her gated

community. Round and round—
I help her find her phone, her keys,

her phone, her keys.
This new math—

My Mother Tells Me Stories

An aunt who entertained priests,
    If you know what I mean she says,

a grandfather who commuted
    between a mistress in Montreal

and the wife he got pregnant
    thirteen times—once for each trip

back home to Lowell.
    My mother corners me in her kitchen

serves up helping after helping—
    her absent dad tried to kidnap

her from Catholic school
    and when she was two his girlfriend

knocked on the door
    to ask, on his behalf, for a divorce.

It's as if she wants to fill me up
    with everything she never told me—

she won the city of Nashua
    spelling bee, sewed her own clothes,

jitterbugged, skied Mad River Glen.
    In her kitchen there's no such thing

as being too full—
    she wanted to be a doctor

ended up a receptionist
    at the Ring Sanitarium, quit

when a drunk threw his whiskey
    in her face—she confesses

it was lonely being an only,
    her mother a nervous wreck,

no father in sight—
    my friends told me to say he died she says.

It's as if she knows
    she is forgetting—

adds too much sugar to the sauce,
    not enough salt—

my job now is to swallow
    every spoonful, relish it.

On the Grain

Because I ignored the bias,
    cut the fabric off-grain

clothes I sewed never fit
    bunched at the knees, pulled

at the hips, pinched at the waist.
    Because I wasn't like my mother

who could hold straight pins
    in her mouth and talk

no matter how hard I tried
    to follow patterns

there were always flaws
    things I should have ripped

out, done over. When she attempted
    to show me, step by step

I was impatient, took shortcuts
    every project failed

to live up to the Simplicity
    pattern-book promises—

skinny-limbed girls in ruched bikinis
    pedal pushers, mother-daughter outfits.

I couldn't make us match. She'd look up
    from her converted treadle,

over the gold letters that spelled SINGER
    wind a bobbin, thread the machine

take her seam ripper
    to my botched hip-hugger miniskirt.

She'd found and flushed
    my drugs. Intercepted and tore up

letters on blue paper from a boy
    I thought I loved.

Why did I think
    I could guess at yardage

fudge seam widths?
    Why did I refuse the seam ripper

only to tear apart what I'd made
    with my hands?

And now she hands me
    this sturdy fabric Mémé wove

in the mills of Lowell.
    I fold it on the grain

warp to warp, weft to weft, place it
    in my basket of remnants.

Ordinary Art

Once you spoke French you say
    and sometimes there was bread, *du pain,*

with milk and sugar
    before bed.

Once there was creamed
    tuna on toast with green peas,

ribbon candy
    that cut your tongue

and later, cigarettes instead of
    lollipops or bubble gum.

Once you believed
    in God you say

then he, *votre père,* walked out
    and your mother

made an ulcer.
    After that it was white bread—

boiled dinners—
    whatever it took

to coat her pain.
    What happens now

as you disappear
    as she did

brain cell by brain cell—
    is that our story?

Predators

One afternoon after another
    an eagle eats at a goose

caught in the frozen
    pond by my office.

We curtain
    the windows, watch

this linebacker of a bird
    dine on ice-kill.

– – – – –

When I come home
    to a screech owl in the rockery

beside the driveway, small
    totem among lamb's ears

and phlox—
    I see it as a sign

that despite two happy owls
    on our anniversary card

perhaps we are headed
    for Splitsville.

– – – – –

I've wandered online
    searching for my lineage,

that unquiet room
    of looms,

the girls who drove them—
    take for instance, my great-grandmother,

née Marie Delorme,
    whose ninety-year story

fits in a thimble—
    dailiness reduced to this

silver and gold
    monogrammed keepsake.

        – – – – –

And my grandmother
    whose county fair afghan,

decades in the making, was disqualified
    by a cross-stitch mistake.

And what of her cracked
    hands,

gloved against blood,
    her bad marriage?

        – – – – –

Is it two
    or three generations to

forgotten—
    still, the way a daughter

walks, a grandson shrugs—
    pure plagiarism, memory muscle

turning backward forward,
    not ours not theirs.

– – – – –

Tell me,
    how will I know

if I'm too far away
    to see what the eagle

leaves behind on the ice?
    In the car, we held

each other's eyes
    in the collapsing light—

I want to know
    how things turn out

although even now
    I'm forgetting them.

If I Forgive You

Red blur of cardinal,
    red flurry, red

something in the corner of my eye—
    I didn't peg you as a killer

of moths
    morning stalker of the loner

who stayed too long
    whose ecru, almost translucent self

hugs the incandescent heat
    of the porch light.

Gorgeous one,
    red beyond belief one,

who imitates the hummingbird
    standing still in midair

through a trickery of wings,
    your thrum quickens my morning—

your scarlet flush
    your fluorescent protection

an epiphany of sorts—
    designed

to find a mate, procreate
    and now you are here

problem-solving for their hunger—
    it's not your fault,

it's how I see you
    in this light, in this moment

before you shapeshift
    back to bird.

Just in Time

How strange to begin to know her now
    as moon, as crescent,

shows herself
    like a cutout,

a negative space
    that is not

after all this time, that is not
    too late, that is just in time,

here, now, at the end, not
    too late, still time

just enough
    as she wanes

each night's sliver,
    brighter.

Notes

"How It Resists" is inspired by *Letters from Susan* from *The Lowell Offering: Writings by Mill Women 1840–1945*, edited by Benita Eisler, J. B. Lippincott Company, 1977, pp. 44–62.

"Great Red Wall" is inspired by lines from the poem "the stars like" by Paul Marion (quoted in *The Belles of New England*, by William Moran, Thomas Dunne Books, St. Martin's Press, 2002, p. 139) and by visits to the Waltham and Boott Cotton mills.

"Theft" borrows lines and is inspired by *A Weaver's Reverie*, from *The Lowell Offering: Writings by Mill Women 1840–1945*, op.cit., pp. 137–138.

"How a Community of Women" borrows the line ". . . sucked thread through the eye of the foot-long wooden shuttles that fed the thread to the looms" from *The Belles of New England*, op.cit, pp. 22–23.

"Coming to Massachusetts" is inspired by and emulates Susan Rich's poem, "Go West, Young Woman" from *The Alchemist's Kitchen*, White Pine Press, 2010.

"Triptych: Travaux d'Aiguille" is inspired by Emilia Phillips' poem, "Triptych: Automata" from *Signaletics*, The University of Akron Press, 2013.

"Thirteen Hours of Labor Daily" is inspired by "A Description of Factory Life by an Associationist in 1846." Source: The Illinois Labor History Society Web Site. http://222.kentlaw.edu/ilhs/lowell.html.

"After the First Week" is inspired by *The Spirit of Discontent*, from *The Lowell Offering: Writings by Mill Women 1840–1945*, op.cit, pp. 160–162. Also informed by *Loom & Spindle or Life Among the Early Mill Girls* (1898), by Harriet Hanson Robinson, Chapter II; http://www.millmuseum.org/history/sweat-of-their-brows/mill-girls/

"Regulations to Be Observed by All" is a found poem from *Factory Rules from the Handbook to Lowell* (1848).

"Dear Francis Cabot Lowell" is inspired by and borrows lines composed by Lucy Larcom: "When I've thought what soil the cotton-plant / We weave is rooted in, what waters it— / The blood of souls in bondage— I have felt / That I was sinning against the light to stay / And turn the accursed fibre into cloth."

"Lowell Cloth Narratives" is inspired by Ex-Slave Narratives conducted by the Works Progress Administration (WPA) in the 1930s. http://library.uml.edu/clh/All/Lowcl.htm.

"Accent" epigraph source: Commonwealth of Massachusetts, *Twelfth Annual Report of the Bureau of Statistics of Labor* (Boston: Rand, Avery, & Co., 1881), pp. 469–470.

Acknowledgments

Grateful acknowledgement is made to the following publications in which these poems, or versions of these poems, first appeared.

AGNI: "Dear Francis Cabot Lowell"

Chiron Review: "Ordinary Art"

Crab Creek Review: "Curating My Grandfather"

The Fem: "My Mother Is Forgetting"

The Human: "Theft"

The Journal: "French Seams"

Michigan Quarterly Review: "How It Resists"

The Mom Egg Review: "On the Grain"

Night Train: "Breakfast on the Lanai with My Mother"

Off the Coast: "Great Red Wall," "Thimbleful"

Potomac Review: "After the First Week"

Room Magazine: "Drawn," "Coming to Massachusetts"

Sou'wester: "How a Community of Women"

3 Nation Anthology: "How a Community of Women"

Valparaiso Poetry Review: "Sewing Lessons"

VAYAVYA: "This Threshold He Did Not Carry Her Across," "The Other Woman"

Yellow Chair Review: "Absent," "Like Her"

Zone 3: "Earthlings," "Notions," "Field Trip: Boott Cotton Mills"

I am grateful to the Salem Writers Group; the Bread Loaf Writers' Conference, in particular Emilia Phillips and Linda Bierds; and to CavanKerry Press, Joan Cusack Handler, Starr Troup, and Baron Wormser. Thank you to Susan Rich for her attention, care, and invaluable help with the collection. I would also like to especially thank Kevin Carey, John Harn, Elisabeth Weiss Horowitz, Jennifer Jean, Jennifer Colella Martelli, Colleen Michaels, January Gill O'Neil, Dawn Paul, Danielle Jones-Pruett, J. D. Scrimgeour, Karen Skolfield, and Margaret Young for their careful reading of many of the poems in this collection, for their camaraderie and community. Thank you also to my first teachers Charles Aukema and Ralph Salisbury and to dear lifelong friends Jane, Carol, and Cynthia. With love and gratitude to my siblings—Carson and Cathy, who were always there with unwavering support, and Cheryl, Carrie, and Carter for inspiring me in so many ways. Thank you to my mother for the stories that inform this collection and to my father for his love of literature and for always believing. Deepest love to my children, Carson and Ketner, whose love and support make all things possible.

CavanKerry's Mission

CavanKerry Press is committed to expanding the reach of poetry to a general readership by publishing poets whose works explore the emotional and psychological landscapes of everyday life.

Other Books in the Emerging Voices Series

Gloved Against Blood was set in the typeface Quadraat OT, which was designed by Dutch type designer Fred Smeijers for the FontFont type foundry between 1992 and 2011.